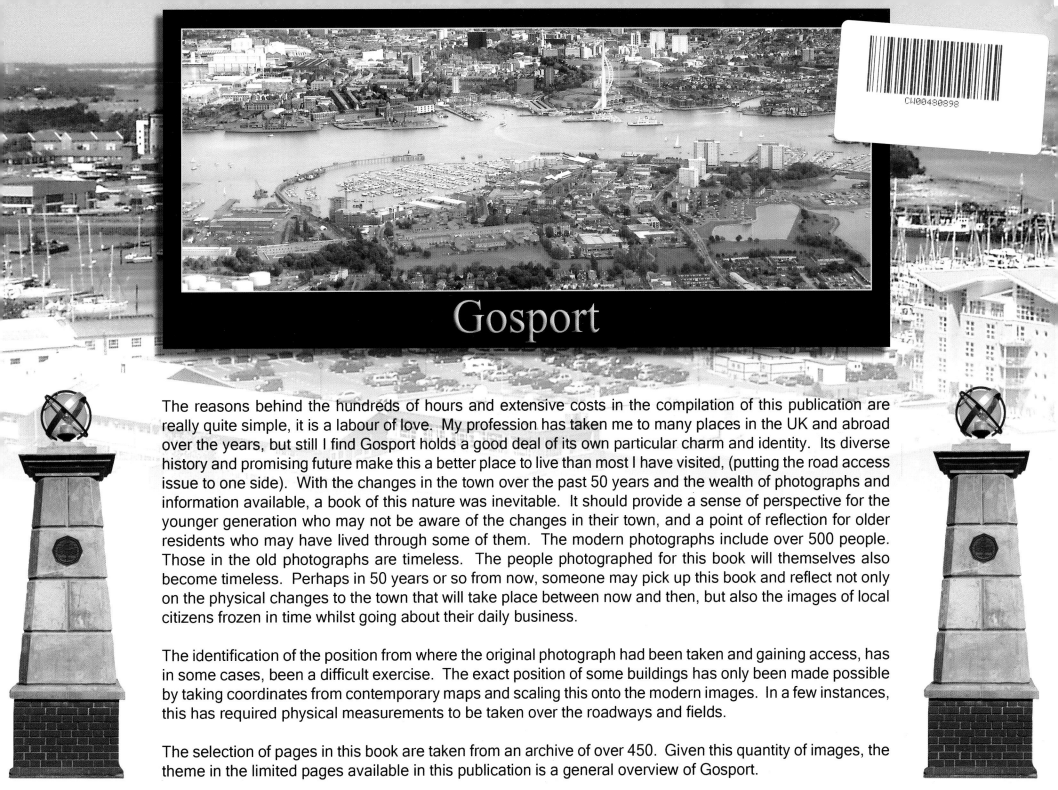

Gosport

The reasons behind the hundreds of hours and extensive costs in the compilation of this publication are really quite simple, it is a labour of love. My profession has taken me to many places in the UK and abroad over the years, but still I find Gosport holds a good deal of its own particular charm and identity. Its diverse history and promising future make this a better place to live than most I have visited, (putting the road access issue to one side). With the changes in the town over the past 50 years and the wealth of photographs and information available, a book of this nature was inevitable. It should provide a sense of perspective for the younger generation who may not be aware of the changes in their town, and a point of reflection for older residents who may have lived through some of them. The modern photographs include over 500 people. Those in the old photographs are timeless. The people photographed for this book will themselves also become timeless. Perhaps in 50 years or so from now, someone may pick up this book and reflect not only on the physical changes to the town that will take place between now and then, but also the images of local citizens frozen in time whilst going about their daily business.

The identification of the position from where the original photograph had been taken and gaining access, has in some cases, been a difficult exercise. The exact position of some buildings has only been made possible by taking coordinates from contemporary maps and scaling this onto the modern images. In a few instances, this has required physical measurements to be taken over the roadways and fields.

The selection of pages in this book are taken from an archive of over 450. Given this quantity of images, the theme in the limited pages available in this publication is a general overview of Gosport.

Harbour Front

One of the ferries that provided extensive service over the years, the Vadne, which was built in 1939, sadly lies rusting today on the shores of Weevil Creek.

Reflections

GOSPORT FERRY AREA, 1935.

The old-hand coloured postcard provides a good deal of information about the ferry area at this time.

One of the two most powerful battleships of the day, H.M.S. Nelson (built 1927, scrapped 1948), is entering harbour for the 1935 Fleet Review. Its crew of 1,716 men shortly to descend on the town. It was run aground near Southsea only the year before, which caused a sensation. The vehicular chain ferry (which ceased operation in 1959) is visible on the extreme right at a site now occupied by the bus station. The old bus station is clearly evident to the lower left of the picture. The white building with the tiled roof was demolished in the 1970's.

The original photograph was taken from the roof of the Market House building, which was on the site now occupied by The Waterfront public house.

Trinity Green

A contributor to this book, Elsie Oakes lived at Number 7 Chapel Row as a child. It can be seen on the map below.

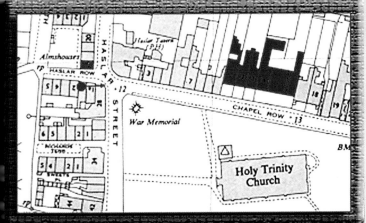

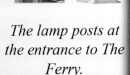

The lamp posts at the entrance to The Ferry.

Reflections

CHAPEL ROW, 1965.

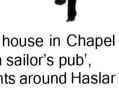

The much photographed Haslar Tavern public house in Chapel Row, which is today Trinity Green. It was very much a sailor's pub', being the first on the route from the Naval establishments around Haslar to the many public houses in the town centre and the last on the way back.

Note the power station chimney in Portsmouth and the old wall to the right which surrounded Trinity Church. Only the houses which were set back from the road remain in the old photograph. Also, the edge of one of the Alms Houses, number 26 Haslar Street can be seen on the extreme left of the picture. These houses are highlighted in red on the map.

The position for re-shooting the scene was achieved by taking the shot from a ladder as the original building from where the old photograph was taken no longer exists.

Trinity Green

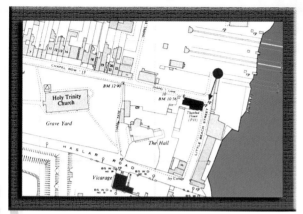

Reflections

BEACH STREET, 1959.

The Thatched House public house, was on the corner of Chapel Lane and Little Beach Street, both of which no longer exist. Its location today would be at the harbour end of Trinity Green, on the right if looking out to the harbour. This photograph was complex to re-create. It was managed eventually after several photo shoots and re-visits. By referencing the end of Chapel Street on an old map of Gosport and scaling this from the distance from Holy Trinity Church, the precise location was determined. The reference is the Vicarage, shown in red on the map, which remains in the background, behind the trees on the right. The Thatched House is shown in blue on the map. The original Thatched House public house was closeby. It was previously named The Block and Block and was demolished to be replaced by the building featured here. The old photograph was taken from a ship under repair on the Camper & Nicholson slipways in Little Beach Street. The Thatched House was popular with American Soldiers in World War II.

The Sundial Area on the Millenium Walk is partially visible on the left.

The old Vicarage can be seen in both photographs

Trinity Green

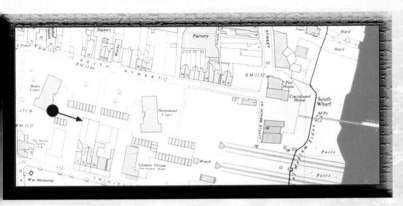

Reflections

TRINITY GREEN, 1959.

A rare, atmospheric view of the Trinity Green area just before the major re-development carried out in the early 1960's. The view shown is actually two photographs blended together, resulting in a panoramic view taken from the top of Blake Court flats.

Key points are, from left to right, the slipway for ship building and repair by Camper & Nicholson (also shown from another angle in the photograph below). The Thatched House public house is in the centre, it is the building with the tall chimney stacks.

The Hall, which was the residence of Mr Nicholson of Camper & Nicholson, is just visible beyond the trees. The Vicarage (now a private residence), is on the extreme right in both photographs.

The photograph on the previous page was taken from a ship being built on the slipway in the distant left in the view below.

The east end of the roof of Trinity Church is just above and to the right of a row of roof tops in Chapel Row, (now Trinity Green).

The road running along the harbour front from left to right, was Beach Street which ran on into Little Beach Street. Part of the street can be seen beyond the Thatched House public house..

Trinity Green

Reflections

TRINITY CHURCH, APRIL 1932.

This wonderfully atmospheric photograph on a rainy, winter's day is completed by the character in the hat lurking in the entrance of the Haslar Tavern public house. The dismounted cyclist talking to a pedestrian in Chapel Row (now Trinity Green) and the youngster running around the corner, possibly to meet a friend leaning against the wall of the church add a storyline. Judging by the activity in this photograph, with the experience gained in settiing up similar shots today, it would appear that the participants have been posed. Today, this level normal activity of people going about their daily business is very difficult to replicate. We mostly seem to be just walking to and from our cars.

Haslar Street running from the right was a few yards closer to the church when the old photograph was taken. This difference can be seen when comparing the two views and the dog-leg in the road on the map.

The War Memorial, which is located inside the graveyard in the old photograph, has been relocated to a position on the right, just outside of the views shown here.

Trinity Green

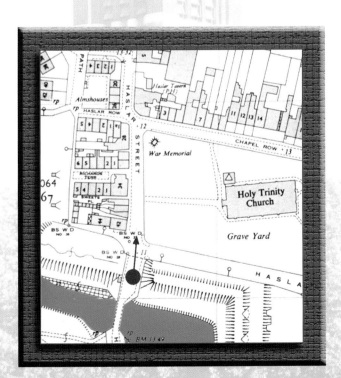

Reflections

HASLAR STREET LOOKING NORTH, 1949.

The Haslar Tavern can be seen at the end of the road. The edge of the old rampart wall is on the left. The railings on the right are unchanged. The wall surrounding Trinity Church has long gone. Children would hide behind this wall at night with bedsheets over their heads, jumping up to frighten the WRNS (Women's Royal Naval Service) on their way back to Haslar.

This part of the old ramparts (Number 1 Bastion) is thankfully still in place. It was known as Vicar's Bank to many generations of amorous youngsters.

The gate through the ramparts was in this location.

Haslar Street

Reflections

3 & 5 HASLAR STREET, 1959.

This superb old Georgian building was in a state of poor repair shortly before demolition. Sadly, it did not survive the post-war clear-out of the Trinity Green area.

This building was located on the east side of Haslar Street adjacent to Flux's Laundry. It looks to have originally been one house, but at the time of the photograph, it was divided into two houses, numbers 3 and 5 Haslar Street. The additional entrance can be seen on the right of the building. Another indicator is the difference in the window styles between the two halves of the house. The last tenants were W. Abbey at number 3 and Lilian Jackson at number 5. The house in this photograph is empty, awaiting the bulldozers. It appears in several old photographs of Gosport, particularly looking east from the swimming pool. An example is the small view at the top of the page. The modern wall, which surrounds a newly built block of flats in 1959, Winchfield House, is a good reference for identification of the location for the original photograph. The road leading in to the middle of the photograph from the right is Church Path.

The wall is all that remains

View from Church Path to Haslar Street.

South Street

Reflections

SOUTH STREET MOAT, 1956.

The moat ran across the path of South Street, then turned left, past the location where Burger King is today.

The fine row of Georgian buildings in Portland Place are easily recognisable in the centre of the picture. The first house on the left in the row was used as temporary offices for the Town Council after World War II due to the loss of the Town Hall to bombing in 1941. South Street today runs between the buildings of Portland Place and the building on the left, which was then the Employment Exchange and is today a dental practice. Just to the left of Trinity Church spire, the houses in Church Path can be seen, although they are not visible in the modern photograph. The Employment Exchange building and Trinity Church tower are all that remain. These can be seen in the small picture for reference.

The small view was taken in the winter to reveal the reference building (The Employment Exchange), behind the trees.

The map provides information on where South Street now runs in relation to the location of the moat.

The route of South Street today is shown in yellow on the map. The Employment Exchange and Portland Place are in red.

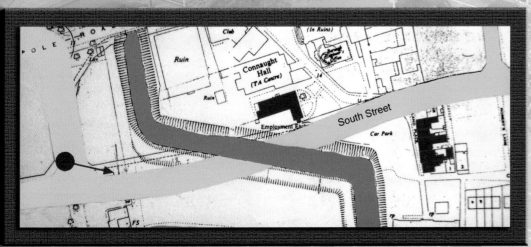

South Street

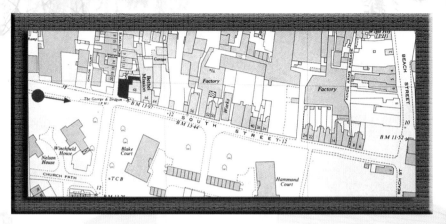

Reflections

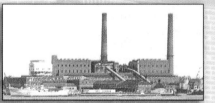

REDEVELOPMENT,
1960.

It is evident that a good deal of change has taken place in South Street since this picture was taken.

The chimney stacks from the power station in Portsmouth dominated the backdrop to this scene for many years, but these have now gone, their place on the skyline taken over by a worthy successor in The Spinnaker Tower.

Blake Court flats are under construction on the right. All that remains on the left of the picture is the George And Dragon pubic house. It is shown in the inset view and in red on the map. The road has been widened considerably on the right.

An interesting reference point, highlighting the passage of time, is the forked path in the grass on the right. The sapling at the apex of the fork has grown into a mature tree of about 60 years old.

Bemister's Lane
Reflections

BEMISTER'S LANE, 1960.

Bemister's Lane was the main thouroughfare to Gosport Common over 300 years ago. At that time horses and carts would be using this lane for access. It was also an area for press gang activity in the 18th and 19th centuries, as stated in the plaque above. The buildings to the right of the lane have mostly survived, with just a few exceptions. On the left, beyond the lane, the area has been cleared to make provision for a car park. It is evident from these old elevated photographs of the area around South Street that the renovation of this area, which began in the late 1950's, was a major improvement to the town. It is just a pity that the bulldozers demolished so many Georgian buildings of historic value that would be so pleasing to the eye today.

Bemister's Lane today represents the only surviving example of the 104 alleyways of old Gosport.

The Lake

The original photograph was taken from the roof of the boat storage wooden hut. To get the angle correct for the re-shoot, the modern photograph was taken from the top of a step ladder as the hut no longer exists.

Older residents may recall the shout from the boat hirer, "come in boat number..." Many pretended they could not hear him to extend their time on the water.

Reflections

THE BOATING LAKE, *c.*1950.

The three storey Georgian houses on the left were in Portland Place. The second house from the right is shown in the smaller view and is highlighted in red on the map. These houses were bomb damaged in World War II and eventually demolished to be replaced with the block of flats that are named after this street. Next along is the chimney from Flux's Laundry in Haslar Street in the distance, followed by a single chimney from the Portsmouth Power Station.
The west end of the old swimming pool is directly below the spire of Trinity Church.

The Swimming Pool

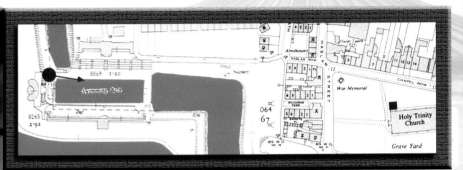

Reflections

THE OPEN AIR SWIMMING POOL, 1968.

Gosport Swimming Pool was opened in 1927. It was formed from a section of the moat which surrounded the town at that time.

The dimensions of the pool were 67 metres (220ft) long by 17 metres (57 ft) wide. It was closed in 1981.

The buildings in the background are unchanged from the 1960's photograph. The only exception being the two chimney stacks from Portsmouth Power Station, which are visible to the left of Trinity Church Tower in the old photograph. The tower is highlighted in red on the map.

The remains of the sun terrace, where so many local people spent a good deal of their summer days, is today a grass bank to the left of the car park.

The end was in sight for this open air pool when the indoor heated pool was opened at Holbrook in 1976.

It was a sad day when the pool closed as it was more than just a place to swim.

Walpole Park

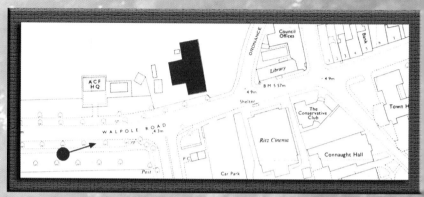

Note the trees. The growth of 80 years or so, is evident. The shape of the branches has provided an excellent reference point for the re-creation of this photograph.

Reflections

WALPOLE PARK LOOKING EAST, 1926.

On the extreme left, just behind the trees, was the Territorial Army Hall, (shown in the small view and in red on the map), which in later years was used as the Driving Examination Centre before demolition in 1989. Looking across the view, the old library and school is in the distant centre. On the far right is a flat area surrounded by wire fencing. This would be the site of The Ritz Cinema, which would be built in just a few years time from the taking of the old photograph.

The boy on the far pavement, across the road, is holding what looks to be a school satchel and a football. He is in Grammar school uniform and posing for the camera. He may have been known to the cameraman, or just a passer by taking the opportunity to be immortalised on film.

The High Street (West End)

The sign above the entrance

1901

WEST END OF THE HIGH STREET *c.*1950.

Reflections

The Technical Institute and Public Library are the main subjects of the old photograph. The building opened on 25th September 1901, at a cost of £6,000. It is now the local studies part of the Discovery Centre, which has been a key source of material for this book.

The front edge of the Ritz Cinema can be seen to the right of the old photograph. This opened in 1934. It was severly damaged by bombing in 1941 during World War II and stood derelict for some time after. It was returned to its former glory in the 1950's but succombed to financial pressures and closed in 1999.

The moat, which was part of the old town defence system originating from Napoleonic times, can be seen passing under a bridge on the High Street.

The map shows part of a road scheme that did not materialise, but the roundabout area is similar in design to the current section of road from South Street to Walpole Road. The moat and bridge can be seen on the map along with the Ritz Cinema, which is highlighted in red.

The High Street
Reflections

THE BELL PUBLIC HOUSE, 1971.

The Bell was on the corner of the High Street and North Cross Street. It was originally called The Old Blue Bell, (but was shortened to The Bell). It was one of the oldest public houses in Gosport.

It is shown here just prior to demolition as part of the major redevelopment of the North Cross Street area.

It is interesting to note on the map, which dates from the 1950's, the number of buildings marked as "In Ruins" which are clearly the effects of wartime bombing.

The building on the left is the reference point for the re-shoot position.

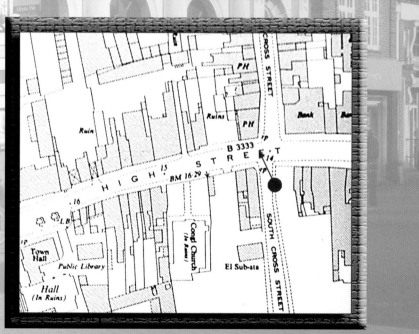

North Street

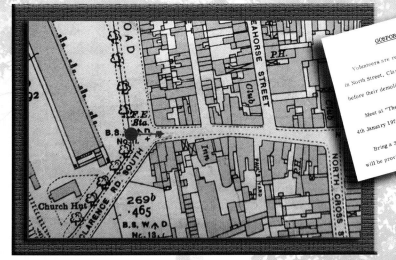

Reflections

NORTH STREET FROM CLARENCE ROAD, MAY 1910

A military parade for the proclamation of King George V. passes Mr. Gluning's newsagents shop on the corner of King's Street and North Street as it heads towards The Thorngate Hall. North Street was a major shopping area in the town which extended right down to the Ferry. The Crown Hotel, which dates from 1750, can be seen on the right and is visible in the modern photograph. It has been renovated after fire damage in 1984. One of the inset views shows a stone which is located inside the arch through to the old ballroom at the rear of the hotel. It is dated 1813. The other inset is the top stone to a time capsule located in the courtyard to the rear of The Crown Hotel building. It is the only surviving building from the old scene, the rest having been demolished in the early 1970's. The map provides an indication as to housing density. During the early part of the nineteenth century there were around 6,000 people within the town's ramparts.

At the top, is a note asking for volunteers to photograph the area before major re-development in 1975.

CROWN MEWS

ON THIS DAY THE 16TH DECEMBER 1988 THE RIGHT WORSHIPFUL THE MAYOR OF GOSPORT COUNCILLOR H. A. B. NICHOLLS PLACED A CAPSULE CONTAINING DOCUMENTS REFLECTING THIS SITE AND THE TIMES IN WHICH WE LIVE. THIS TO BE RETRIEVED ONLY BY THE MAYOR OF GOSPORT ON THE 16TH DECEMBER 2088

Clarence Road South

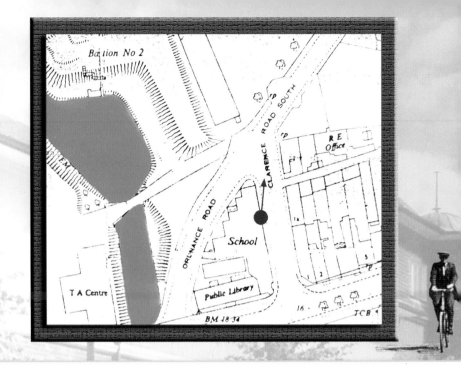

Reflections

CLARENCE ROAD LOOKING FROM THE MUSEUM, 1949.

The trees provide good reference points to re-create the position of the original shot. They are exhibiting the growth of over 55 years. St George's Barracks, now a housing complex, is visible behind the trees.

The old house on the right corner has long gone, but is a good indicator of the type of housing around this area at the time. The site was a car park in the intervening period between the old house being demolished and the apartments being built.

Seahorse Street

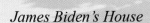

James Biden's House

Reflections

SEAHORSE STREET, 1972.

This area was completely redeveloped just after the old photograph was taken. It is now Seahorse Walk. On the left in the new photograph, the bow window which is behind the climbing plant belongs to the house purchased in 1846 by the local Brewer, James Biden. His brewery was on the opposite side of this street. On the right are cottages from the same period. They used to adjoin The Seahorse public house. The houses remaining today are shown on the map in red.
The Elite Club signposted on the old building to the left, was anything but in its final years.

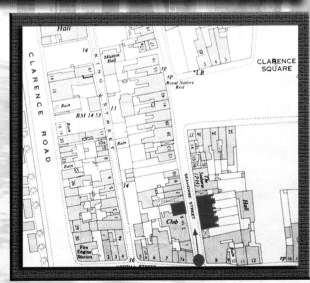

Clarence Road

Part of the Clarence Tavern public house, a lone survivor from times gone by.

The building on the left was originally Clarence Hall. It was converted to The Masonic Hall in 1928

Reflections

CLARENCE ROAD LOOKING SOUTH, 1910.

In the far distance of the old photograph, beyond the end of the street, can be seen the rear of the Thorngate Hall and a small part of the Town Hall. The central overhead cable stanchions for the tramway can be seen in the centre of the road. All that remains today of this once densely populated area is the Masonic Hall, which is on the left of the photograph and the Clarence Tavern public house, which is at the entrance to the road and not in this view. The top of the Masonic Hall has been modified, but the lower section is much the same as it was with the exception of the attractive lamp over the replacement door and the modern windows. Mr. Mill's boot and shoe repair shop can be seen half way along the road. Beyond this was Sandecombe's wholesale newspaper distributer. The awning further along was over Mrs Evan's sweet shop.

There were many alleyways between the buildings through to King's Street.

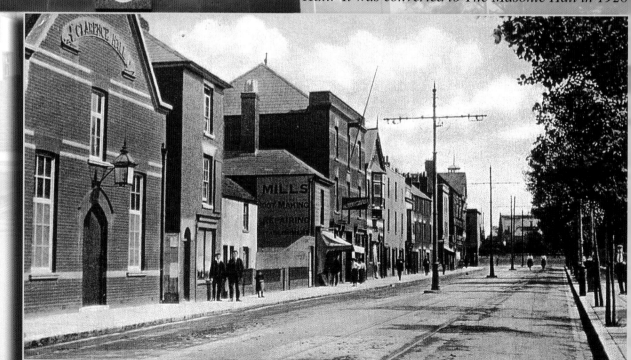

Clarence Road
Reflections

LOOKING NORTH, 1949.

A point of note is that the tram overhead support pylons are still in place despite the tram having been taken out of service 20 years earlier. The absence of tramlines in the road bear witness to this. The Masonic Hall can be seen in the distance on the right hand side of the road. It is the only visible building remaining today. It is marked in red on the map.
The Fire Station is partially in view on the right. It was on the corner of North Street. When it was demolished, the service was relocated to Bury Cross..

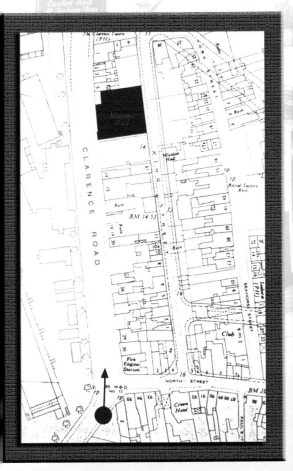

A. Millard MILLER
The Corn Stores, 30 Clarence Rd., Gosport. Tel. 8492.
Corn, Hay and Straw Merchant.
All Kinds of Bird Seed.

This view, taken in 1972 shows the last of the type of shops along this road. The shop at the centre is Alan Millard's Corn Store. How many shop today could trade solely on the range of products advertised?

Mumby Road

Reflections

MUMBY ROAD END OF CLARENCE ROAD, 1959.

At first glance the new photograph looks to be an advertisement for the new development at Rope Keys, but the history around this area is quite extensive.

The old photograph shows St Matthew's Square not long before demolition in 1959 to make way for the Mumby Road development. The old photograph can be referenced by looking at the extreme right. The very edge of the Clarence Tavern, which was originally called The Blue Anchor until the mid' 19th century, is just visible as a white vertical band. The decorative edging towards the top is a good indicator. The function room at the rear was added later. The Duke of Cornwall public house is directly ahead. It's location would be right in the middle of Mumby Road today. To the left is Kistle's general store and newsagent. Ahead, through the gap between the buildings can be seen an old car. This is parked outside of Rocky Norman's yard. Just around the corner in York Street, is the edge of the Mitre Tavern public house. The housing in the area ahead was of a very low standard. Mount Street was dingy and Kent's Alley, which was behind the Vicarage, (shown in red on the map), had hovels with no running water, only a shared standpipe in the centre of the alley.

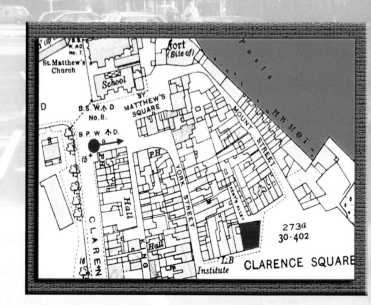

Clarence Square

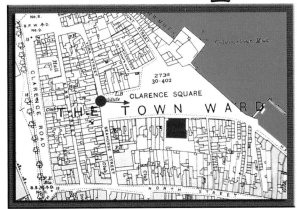

Reflections

CLARENCE SQUARE, c.1910.

Clarence Square School is highlighted in this view.

The old photograph was taken on the corner of York Street (long gone), as it entered the Square, which was more of a triangle in reality.

HMS Victory will be still afloat in the harbour for another 10 years before going into dry dock in Portsmouth.

What a fine area this must have been at this time. The Georgian houses on the right, had unspoiled views across the north of the Harbour. Clarence Square School, built in 1907, which is just to the right of the cart and can be referenced on the contemporary map, is still there today although not as a school. It is behind the tree in the modern photograph. The school was the only survivor of the WW II bomb damage and the 1950/60's developers.

The old Vicarage was to the left of the photograph, just out of sight. It can be seen on the map as an open walled area. It was said to be haunted. The houses on the harbour shore, in Mount Street, had their back yards open to the sea. The high tide would send water up to the back doors. The large building on the left was originally the sail loft for Ratsey & Lapthorn. It was built in Clarence Square after the original building, closer to Camper & Nicholson, was destroyed by WWII bombing.

The High Street

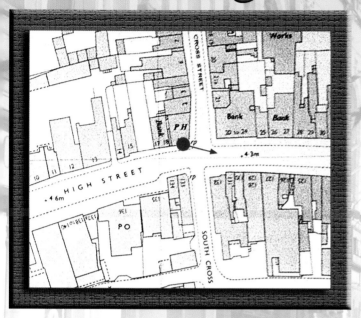

THORNTON THEATRE

From 1796 to 1826, this building housed the Gosport Theatre, owned and managed by the actor-manager Henry Thornton, who built the original Theatre Royal at Windsor for George III

Unveiled by Councillor Aleck Hayward
Mayor of Gosport
2001

The plaque on the front of the Thornton Theatre. This is the building with the brick front and apex roof.

Reflections

HIGH STREET, c.1935.

The original photograph was taken from the first floor, which was the living room of The Bell public house.

The length of the shadows on the south side, which are visible on the road, are a good indicator of the time of day and season in which the photograph was taken. The modern photograph has almost the same shadow pattern. This was taken at 1.15pm in late October. The original photograph appears to have been taken at the same time of the year, but slightly later in the day as the shadow angle is in a more advanced orientation. Judging by the lack of shoppers, the day is probably a week day. The buildings have barely changed at all over the intervening 70 years between shots.

The shops in the old photograph from right to left looking down the High Street, are: A Hooper (Wet Fishmonger), Scotch Wool Shop, Pinks (General Store), Timothy White's (General Store), Harvey's (Tobacconist), Maypole (Grocery Shop), Dorothy Cooper (Hat Shop).

St. George Barracks

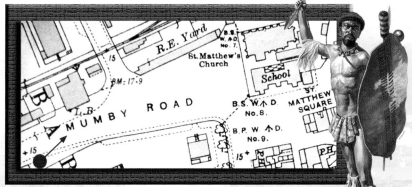

Reflections

THE NEW BARRACKS GUARDHOUSE, *c.*1905.

This was completed in 1858, at very high cost for the time.
The sapling in front of the Guardhouse has grown extensively in 100 years. It is a good comparator by which to estimate the age of trees around the town. Tram lines score across the lower portion of the picture. The overhead power line for the tram can just be seen at the upper right of the photograph. Just beyond the picture to the right would be St Matthews Church and School. The very edge of this church is just visible behind and above the man on the far right of the new photograph, who is duplicated from the picture above. It is marked in red.
The Rope Keys apartment development is underway in the background.

THE ZULU CONNECTION.

After the battle at Rourke's Drift in 1879, during the Zulu War in South Africa, the unit involved, the 1st Battalion, 24th Regiment, was stationed in Gosport at St George Barracks on it's return to England. How many film goers in 1963 sat in The Ritz Cinema watching the film "Zulu", which was based on this battle, could imagine that the persons involved were stationed just a few yards behind them 83 years previously?

The High Street

Reflections

The entrance to the High Street in the old photograph bears little resemblance to the view today. The Isle of Wight Hoy public house is on the extreme left and the King's Arms is the white building three places further along. On the right are the remains of the Market House, having been bombed in World War II. Behind this is the Old Northumberland public house. It has a large Watneys sign on the roof, no doubt taking advantage of the loss of the upper story of the Market House, which would have previously obscured the view.

The reference points are the buildings containing Woolworths & New Look. It seems that they have changed very little today from their appearance in the old photograph.

The entrance to the Dive Cafe can be seen on the far right. It is below the Hants & Dorset sign.

The Gambier Drinking Fountain has been installed in several locations around the entrance to Gosport from the ferry over the years. It features in many old photographs.

The High Street

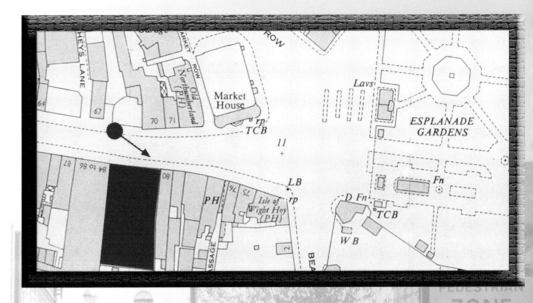

Littlewoods, now New Look, is shown in red on the map. The King's Arms public house is identified as "PH"

Reflections

THE HIGH STREET, THURSDAY 1st JUNE, 1961.

The subject of the old photograph is clearly the buildings that were to be lost in the forthcoming redevelopment of this area. The shadows cast by the cars indicate that it is around midday, so the lack of passers-by is a mystery. The original Port Hole fish & chip shop is next door. The remainder of the buildings to the Isle of Wight Hoy public house at the end were all demolished. The area above Contessa, (a fireplace is visible), was bombed during World War II and not replaced. The left hand window in the upper floor of Littlewoods has been removed. Close inspection of the right hand Littlewoods window reveals the reflection of The Old Northumberland public house across the road. The cars in view are, from the left to right, Austin Cambridge, MG Magnet ZB and the ubiquitous Morris Minor, (probably green in colour), with Portsmouth registration number plates.

The High Street

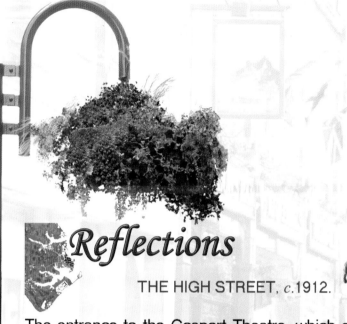

Reflections

THE HIGH STREET, c.1912.

The entrance to the Gosport Theatre, which served as one of the town's earliest cinemas, can be seen on the right in the old photograph. It had only been open for two years when this photograph was taken. A genuine entrance ticket is shown on the right. The building was previously a chapel.

The time of day is late afternoon in the Spring or Autumn judging by the length of the shadows and the attire of the people.

The tramlines, as in many photographs of the time, are visible. It is of note that the boy with the bicycle can stand to pose in the centre of the road without any fear of vehicles.

The buildings on the near right are still intact, but looking further down on the left, many have all been replaced. Most of these were lost to bombing in World War II.

Note the sunshades on the south facing shop windows and the horse droppings in the road which were probably not an unusual sight at the time.

The High Street

Reflections

THREE VIEWS.

The old black and white photograph is *c.*1905. The old Town Hall can be seen to the right. On the left, the two buildings are much the same today. Number 4 High Street is the building with the arched tops to the windows. It was originally the premises of the Gosport Waterworks Company. The 1982 view with the red Mini car, still has the main road running through the town centre. The latest view shows the effect of the pedestrianisation scheme, the Saturday market being a beneficiary of the increased space created by the scheme.

The Town Hall

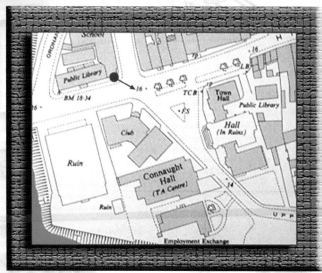

Reflections

THORNGATE AND THE TOWN HALL, *c.*1904.

Both photographs of the Town Hall area were taken from a window in the corner tower of the Gosport Museum, which was the spiral staircase to the flat for the caretaker of the school. The angle was difficult to achieve due to the nature of the spiral staircase, which has not changed since the original picture was captured. It is likely that the original photographer had the same problem.

The old Town Hall is to the left. In the centre is Thorngate Hall, which was built in 1885 and demolished in 1963. Thorngate Hall did not survive the attentions of the German Air Force in World War II. An incendiary bomb rendered it a burned out shell in 1941, which it remained until being demolished. The Ritz cinema was similarly damaged in the same bombing raid. These are both identified as ruins on the map.

The Ramparts

Reflections

LOOKING WEST, 1949.

This view taken from the bank of Bastion Number 1 has some interesting points. Looking from left to right, in the distance, the Boating Lake storage shed can be seen. Moving across, the swimming pool's south wall with its pump house is on the grass bank. The Ritz Cinema's back wall and roof protrude above the backdrop of the Swimming Pool. The roof of The Connaught Drill Hall is next along. On the very right, a roof of one of the houses just inside the old rampart wall is visible. In front of this is a rare view of the rampart that was removed to make way for the apartments that are prominent in this view. The old bridge across the moat is just about visible although this old photograph does not show it in detail due to the under exposure in this area. The inset view shows the Royal Marine Light Infantry passing along the road in the photographs, through Haslar Gate into the town in the 1920's.

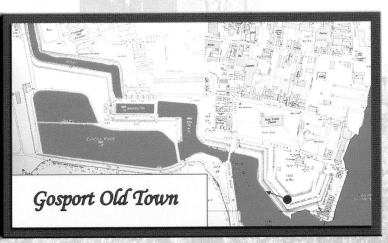

Gosport Old Town

Haslar Bridge

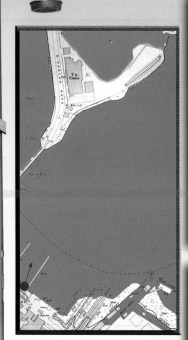

The map indicates the point in time when a toll was levied to cross the bridge. It pre-dates the old photograph.

HASLAR BRIDGE FROM THE HASLAR SIDE, *c.*1960's

Reflections

Many local residents will recall "Pneurnonia Bridge" with mixed feelings. The single track, elevated structure in the old photograph was constructed over the remains of the road bridge built in 1834, which was part of Robert Cruickshank's scheme to get travellers to Angleseyville from the ferry area. The centre span was removed during World War II as a precaution against invasion.

Just over the bridge can be seen part of the Territorial Army Drill Hall building which was demolished to make way for the housing development there in the early 1980's.

Alverstoke Reflections

THE CRESCENT, *c.*1900

Completed in 1828 by Robert Cruick-shank to develop the resort he named Angleseyville, but due to mixed success, only half of the crescent was completed. It is today, just half a crescent. The existing half is shown in red on the contemporary map. The proposed, but not started half is shown in yellow. As can be seen, the space was available at the time for this development.

The contrast in ladies' leisure attire over the 106 year interval period is very evident. Today, a lady jogging in shorts is approaching the spot where her counterpart would dare not enter the street in less than a formal dress at a similar time of day. All she has is her parasol for protection against the midday sun.

Reflections

FROM THE BELL TOWER, ST. MARY'S CHURCH, *c.*1960's.

Looking south, the factory buildings in the foreground have been replaced by houses. A group of town houses has been built in the upper centre of the view. The Stokes Bay seafront buildings, just visible on the distant shoreline, have been demolished to make way for the modern buildings there today.

The journey to the top of the church tower was an interesting one to say the least. Different types of ladders and trapdoors became more precarious as the top was approached. The final exit to the roof space was through a tiny door from a very old iron ladder. Not for the squeamish!

Alverstoke

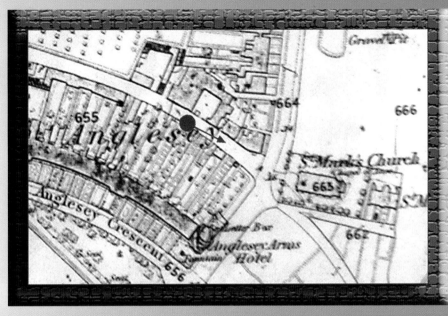

To the left, the sign on the outside of the building is a reminder of it's time as a public house.

Reflections

ANGLESEY ARMS ROAD, *c.*1908

St Mark's Church can be seen in the distance in the old photograph. It was built in 1844 and demolished in 1911 due to structural problems. Today, the old brick wall surrounding the cemetery is still there. It is visible in the distance. The church was constructed as part of Robert Cruickshank's Angleseyville project, which was dominated by The Crescent.

The Anglesey Arms was a public house for a comparatively short period. It was converted into private housing in about 1917. The beer cellar is still in place today.

The shop just visible by the awning on the corner, was reputed to be the point where the train taking Queen Victoria from the Isle of Wight stopped to take on provisions for the journey. The railway line from the pier was just beyond the church.

Stokes Bay

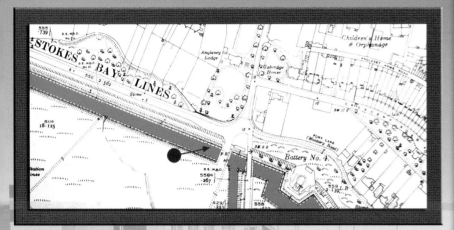

Reflections

STOKES BAY MOAT *c.*1930.

It is probable that most of the people in the new
photograph are not aware that they are passing over the
path of the old moat system that used to extend along
Stokes Bay. The old hand-coloured postcard is that of a
seemingly heathly stretch of water. It was at times
anything but this. The moat can be seen on the map.

The Crescent is clearly visible in it's splendor, although
today, trees and houses mask it from this view.

The reference point is the house just left of centre. There
is another house to the right, just above the bridge over
the moat which today is white. This was in place at the
time of the old photograph being taken. Despite the 70
years that have elapsed between the taking of the
photographs, this area still retains it's attractive character

Stokes Bay

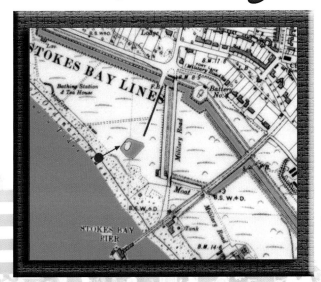

Reflections

BY THE BEACH IN THE 1920's.

The path to the pool can still be seen today.

The children's pool at Stokes Bay was initially a very basic construction. It seemed to be just an excavated area filled with water. It was later converted into a more robust structure. The contemporary map shows the location of the pool clearly, just ahead of the arrow. The old pathway to the pool still exists today in the middle of the grassed area. It is marked in red on the map and can just be seen running across the back of the modern photograph as a brown line. The pool was filled in during the early 1960's due to a polio scare. The house dead ahead with the white apex at the front was used to determine the co-ordinates for the reshoot.

The small view above is that of a family in the same spot in 1930.

Stokes Bay

Stokes Bay Pier.

 ## Reflections

STOKES BAY, *c.*1930's.

The promenade, has changed somewhat over the years. The Tea House on the left was replaced by the modern structure in 1989. The Sailing Club building dominates the scene today. The promenade was widened in 1943 as part of the building work for the construction of the "Mulberry Harbours" for the invasion of France a year later.

In the disctance, on the horizon, Fort Gilkicker can just be seen. The railway pier, constructed in 1842, was originally used for transportation to the Isle of Wight and later taken over by the Admirality. It was demolished in the 1970's

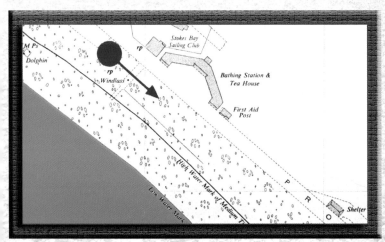

Stokes Bay

Fort Gomer

Reflections

LOOKING EAST FROM THE TOP OF No. 2 BATTERY, 1935.

The waterway to the left is the old moat which formed part of the defence system of Gosport known as the Stokes Bay Lines. This can be seen on the contemporary map. The moat was filled in in the 1950's to provide more leisure space for the growing population of Gosport after World War II.

In the distance can be seen the railway pier which was demolished in the 1970's.

A point of interest is Fort Gomer on the map. This was demolished in the 1960's to make way for the Gomer Estate which is a short distance around the corner to the left.

Above is a Provincial open top bus on its summer route to Fareham along Stokes Bay.

Gosport Park

The oval view shows the tank being installed in the park in 1920.

Reflections

GOSPORT PARK, *c.*1931.

At first sight it appears that little has changed over the 75 years between the taking of the two main photographs. However, on closer examination it can be seen that in the distance the Admiralty Experimental Works, now QinetiQ building at Haslar, has been erected and partly obscures the water tower in Haslar Hospital. The Tennis Courts were only removed in the 1970's. On the left, along the path, the old pavilion is partially visible. The trees, despite 75 years growth, seem surprisingly, not a great deal different. The brach patterns are unchanged.

To the upper right of this page is a cameo comparison of the area where a World War I tank was on display, as was common just after the war. It was a method to make use of the large numbers that had been manufactured but had soon become obsolete. It remained there for many years.

Alverstoke School

The houses shaded in red are on the site of the old school.

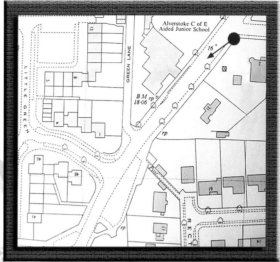

Reflections

ALVERSTOKE SCHOOL, 1972.

The school at Alverstoke was one of the oldest in Gosport. It was teaching children in the middle of the ninteenth century until it's demolition in the 1970's. The houses in the distance on the left are a reference point, as is the surviving tree across the road. It's left hand neighbour was not so lucky. Part of another tree is just visible on the left of both photographs.

Anglesey Gardens
Reflections

ANGLESEY MODEL BOAT POND, 1949.

The houses to the right, behind the bushes are the rear of those located in Linden Grove.

The Gosport Bowling Club has taken over a portion of the reclaimed area. The new greens are behind the trees in the modern photograph.

There is a pathway to the right that provides access from Foster Road through to the path which was part of the old railway line from Stoke Road Station to Stokes Bay.

It is probable that the younger generation of today, when travelling along these pathways have no awareness of the previous incarnation of this cornfield site. It is indicative of the changing leisure pursuits today, that simple pleasures, such as model boating are perhaps on the decline. When this photograph was taken, there was another large model boating lake only a mile away at Walpole Park. This would suggest that demand was high for this type of leisure activity in the early part of the 20th century.

Gosport Bowling Club

Foster Road

Reflections

LOOKING NORTHEAST, c.1920.

Foster Gardens had not yet been constructed and are shown as a blank area on the map. The tram is passing the junction on its way along Foster Road. The route is not as direct as it may have been to the terminus at Bury Cross. The house owners in affluent Bury Road may have had influence with the local authorities as the line construction was diverted along Foster Road rather than the more direct route through Bury Road.

The distinctive houses that dominate the centre of the scene, are largely unchanged today.

The faint view of the building in the far distance, as the road turns left, is the rear of the old White Hart public house.

Linden Grove is the turning on the right. The house which has yet to be built in the vacant position behind the lady in the old photograph is under modification today.

Two local people recreate the poses from the original photograph. As with many of the recreated photographs in this book, the trees provide a living measurement of the elapsed time between shots.

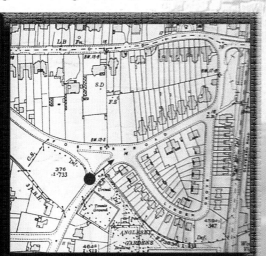

Stoke Road Area

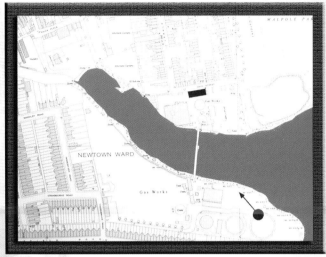

Reflections

THE PARISH OF CHRIST CHURCH, 1962.

The buildings in the old photograph provide fine reference points to place this view. Two, in particular stand out in addition to the churches in Stoke Road. These are highlighted in the small view. The one on the left is now CVS motor repair shop and the terrace on the right, which is derelict in the old photograph (highlighted in red on the map), were the offices of the Gas Company. They are today the offices of TML Chartered Accountants. The remains of the footbridge shown on the map, which linked these offices to the gas storage cylinders can be seen on the old photograph.

The area shown as a tidal inlet was land filled and is now the site occupied by ASDA supermarket and Severnside Recycling.

Both photographs were taken from the top of the gas cylinder as shown on the map. The trek to the top, in 3 degrees Centigrade on a winter's day, was not for the fainthearted. It also required a good deal of co-ordination with the gas company to gain access.

The reference buildings are highlighted.

Stoke Road

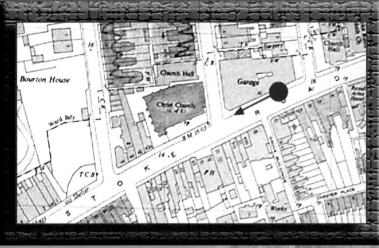

Righton & Bennett garage was to the right of the lady with the white blouse and large hat. Built in the 1920's. As can be seen from the map, it was a large structure. The site is now occupied by Cray House.

Reflections

STOKE ROAD, *c.*1915.

On the left can be seen Richmond Stores at number 49 Stoke Road. This no longer exists and has been replaced by a 1960's development. Some residents may recall the Oasis Steak House being located in the newer building in the 1960's and 70's.

The buildings beyond on the left are generally unchanged in appearance. On the right, on the corner of Elmhurst Road in the distance, stood the large house named Leventhorpe which was erected for Charles Nicholson of Camper & Nicholson yatch building fame. It was demolished to make way for the block of flats that bear its name today.

Christ Church outer wall is just visible on the right in both photographs.

The tramlines weave their way to Bury Cross.

Stoke Road

Reflections

STOKE ROAD, *c*,1909.

This old hand coloured photograph shows the Vine public house on the left. The two carts parked outside provide a sense of context to the view. There were still areas in the vicinity that had a largely agricultural purpose. This is evident by the undeveloped areas on the contemporary map. .

The tram in the photograph is on it's route from the ferry to the terminus at Bury Cross.

The house beyond The Vine is still there today, minus it's chimney stacks.

There were only three buildings on the north side of Stoke Road at the time of the photograph and map. The third was The Union Chapel, which is mentioned on the next page in this book.

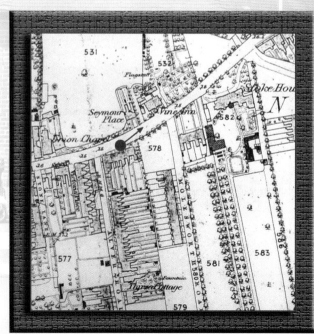

Stoke Road

THE WHITE HART

Reflections

STOKE ROAD, *c.*1920.

The original White Hart public house can be seen in the distant centre. The statue of a White Hart is visible in both views. The building is shown in red on the contemporary map. The Halfway House public house is also shown on the left in the old photograph on the corner of Alver Road.

The gentleman in the foreground adds period atmosphere to the shot. Dressed in a suit with a flat cap and pipe. As with so many old views of the town, sailors in uniform feature among the passers by.

The small view is of Union Chapel, built in 1864. The front railings are just visible on the extreme right behind the trees in the old photograph. The site is now occupied by Marina Buildings. The chapel is shown on the map.

Stoke Road

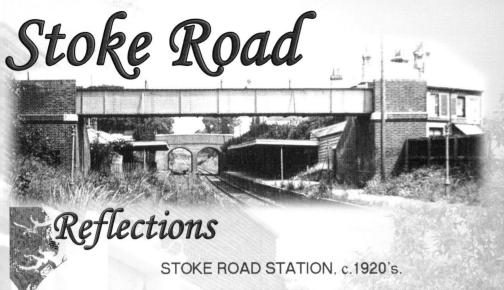

Reflections

STOKE ROAD STATION, c.1920's.

To the right is a rare view of the west side entrance to Gosport (Stoke) Road Railway Station. It is taken from the road to the left of the White Hart public house. This road was called, appropriately, Station Approach and passed through to Cleveland Road.

The line was opened in 1863, the footbridge being erected later in 1889. This side of the station was extended in 1910 to provide more shelter for passengers. The station closed for passenger traffic in 1915, was finally closed altogether in 1936. The bridge with two arches in the distance in the photograph above, provided the means for Bury Road to span the railway line. It was demolished in 1938. The map indicates a footbridge over the railway line as Jacob's Ladder. This is the reference point for the re-shoot of the old photograph. The tops of the houses beyond the footbridge can be seen in the old photograph. They are still there today, although the removal of the footbridge has made them more prominent

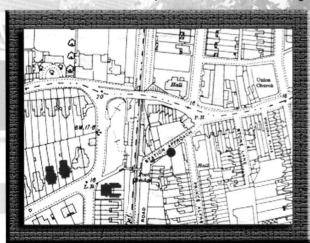

The reference house beyond the footbridge has been cut in half due to the South Relief Road development.

Foster Road

Reflections

FOSTER ROAD FROM LINDEN GROVE, 1914.

This is a scene of traffic free tranquility where the children in the foreground can cross the road, which is free of cars, in relative safety. What does bring a touch of personality to this picture is the older girl lifting the younger one onto the pavement. It is a refreshing departure from many of the staged photographs from this period. The bathchair parked halfway on the pavement adds period atmosphere to the scene.

The tram can be seen just outside the old Stoke Road Station. Appropriately, a bus is in the same position in the modern photograph. This site is now occupied by the telephone exchange. The house on the left remains from the original picture, although the wall at the front is masked by foliage. The house at the end of the road in the top picture also remains, but is not in view in the modern photograph.

Molesworth Road

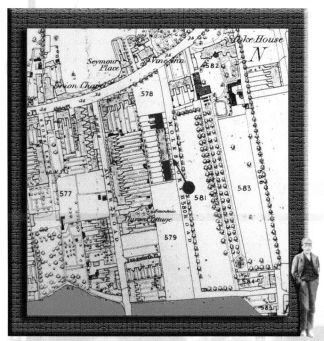

Reflections

MOLESWORTH ROAD, *c.*1910.

The row of houses on the left were known as Brune Terrace. The South Relief Road cut a path through them leaving the four white faced houses that are the main feature in the photograph and two brick faced houses just past the trees further down the road. These are shown in red on the map. The extent of the original terrace can also be seen on the map. To the right in the old photograph, the open tree-lined area with an orchard behind extended down to Workhouse Lake. This placed these houses in a very pleasant location before being completely surrounded by subsequent urban development.

Above right is one of the original boot-scrapers which are still in place by the doorstep of each house in the remainder of the terrace.

Bury Cross

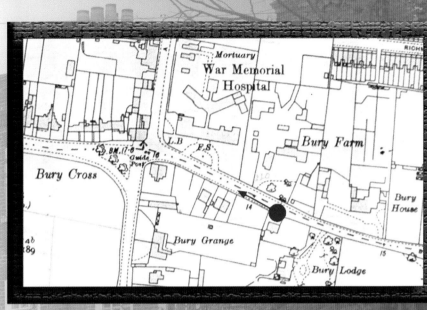

Reflections

BURY CROSS LOOKING WEST, c.1925.

Bury Cross was the end point for the tram system from Gosport town centre. Another route was along Forton Road to Fareham. In the old photograph, the tram has just commenced its journey back to Gosport. The tram did not turn around as such, but was drivable from both ends. The driver would turn the overhead power arm on the tram to face the other direction. The tram ceased operation at the end of 1929.

The Wiltshire Lamb public house is in the distant centre of both photographs. This establishment has featured in many old views of the area. It remains remarkably unchanged over the past 100 years.

The War Memorial Hospital on the right was opened in 1923 as the official World War I memorial to the Royal Marine Light Infantry.

Ann's Hill Road

The 1819 Stone

Bury Cross

Some people may recall my father, Frank Marshall, who was the landlord of The Harvest Home between 1962 and 1972.

Reflections

LOOKING NORTH, 1910.

Ann's Hill Road was a rural area in 1910. This is reflected in the names of the two public houses that were adjacent to each other at the Bury Cross end. The Wiltshire Lamb remains on the corner of the road. The Harvest Home public house, is visible on the left. Major modifications were to result in the structure seen today which has been converted into private dwellings. It was a staging post for horse drawn coaches. A smithy to look after the needs of the horses, was located in what is now a car park. This can be seen on the map.

There is a stone in the back garden wall marked with the date 1819. It is located in the garden of a block of sheltered accommodation which has been built in the previous garden of the Harvest Home. The rear garden was large with many grassed areas and trees, which can be viewed on the old map. The area behind the garden was used for World War I purposes. Excavations in 1969 unearthed many artifacts from this time, including a Vickers heavy machine gun.

St Vincent

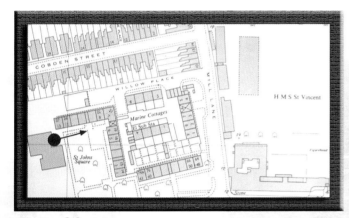

Reflections

LOOKING EAST, 1972.

The old photograph shows H.M.S. St Vincent Boys' Training Establishment just before it was demolished in 1972, to make way for St Vincent Sixth Form College. Some buildings within the complex survived. In addition to the main frontage along Forton road, at the rear, the old canteen and raquet hall with a few other buildings survive today. The canteen contains the reception area for the Leisure Centre. The Raquet Hall is at the entrance to the sports halls. It contains the single Badminton court, as it did in it's prime. The swimming pool was originally an indoor rifle range.

Built in 1847, it was the barracks for the Royal Marine Light Infantry. It became the training centre for entrants into the Royal Navy in 1927. The large white mast in the parade ground was the focal point for celebrations for 5th November. The cadets would scale the mast and stand up in formation on the yard arms, while a cadet would ascend to the platform just below the top.

To the right is the clock tower above the main gate.

Forton Road
Reflections

FORTON ROAD, c.1920.

This view looking east towards Forton Barracks is easily recognised by the clock tower at the entrance. Fortunately, it survives today.

On the left, the old houses that existed before the high rise flats that are there today, can be seen. These houses, unlike their counterparts in Cobden Street behind, had front gardens which were a luxury at the time. The large signboard is for a C. H. Smith, Bootmaker & Repairer, no doubt plying trade from the large numbers of marines stationed next door at Forton Barracks.

There is a tram down the road, which is slightly blurred due to the high exposure times required for cameras of the period. On the right, is the edge of The Victory public house which was demolished in 1978.

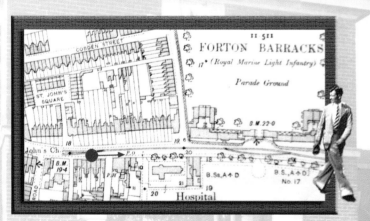

The small photograph shows the view taken from an upper room slightly further down the road, eleven years earlier than the main photograph. It is the Royal Marine Light Infantry Marathon Race. They have just left their barracks at the start of the race, hence the energetic and closely packed runners.

Forton Road

Another photograph of the same event

Reflections

GERMAN PRISONERS IN THE FIRST WORLD WAR.

Two weeks into the First World War, a German merchant vessel entered the Solent area. The ship was attacked by the land based guns and the crew surrendered. After being landed at Yarmouth on the Isle of Wight, the crew of 120 men were transferred to Gosport. They landed at Clarence Yard. From there, they were marched to Fort Elson for imprisonment. The smiling faces of the escorting troops and the children walking alongside are evidence of the naive enthusiasm at the outset of this horrific conflict. It is doubtful that the crowd scene would have been similar if this event had occurred one year later. The only remaining building today is Crossland's Funeral Service. This is highlighted in the small view. The original Queen Charlotte public house can just be seen on the extreme left of the old picture. The Stag public house is just visible in the centre, on the bend. Both are shown in the contemporary map.

All that remains is Crossland's Funeral Home.

Forton Road

All that remains of Lees Lane Prison

Reflections

FORTON ROAD, *c*.1905.

The old Forton Dairy is on the right at number 189. Note the edges of the advertising signs on the extreme right in both photographs. Next to this, with white corner stones, is a building that is of the same design style as Forton Prison, which was located close by, in Lees Lane. It was demolished in the 1920's. It can be matched to one of the remaining buildings from the prison, (marked in red on the contemporary map and shown in the inset view). This is visible from the car park behind the buildings on the right.

The white building further down the road in the old photograph was The Fountain Inn public house. The building today is a barber shop. The old sign area can still be seen on the wall above the entrance.

It is interesting to note the narrow width of the road in the old photograph. It has since been widened to twice its original size.

Forton Road

MILL ROAD
CUL DE SAC

Reflections

THE JUNCTION OF ANN'S HILL ROAD AND FORTON ROAD IN THE 1920's.

The tram can be seen coming into the picture on its journey from the Gosport Ferry to Fareham. On the extreme right in the old photograph is the entrance to the public lavatory that was located on the island in the road junction. There was one similar at the Brockhurst/Elson Road junction.

To the left, but outside the view of the old photograph, a windmill stood derelict for many years over the later part of the 19th Century. Above is a rare picture of that structure. The second map pre-dates the old photograph, but shows the windmill (highlighted in red) and the shoreline of the water that used to run up behind Forton Road from the inlet at St Vincent. Not surprisingly, the road is called Mill Road.

ST ANN'S TERRACE C·1858·B

A plaque indicating the date of construction of the terrace of cottages in the distant centre right.

Brockhurst

Reflections

BROCKHURST, c.1910.

This was a main stopping point for the Gosport to Fareham tram. In addition to local people, soldiers using forts Brockhurst and Elson would use this stop.

The house on the left has changed little over the years. The left section of the terrace next along also remains. It is of a different design to the adjoining houses and was clearly designed for use as a corner shop. To illustrate its diversity it is advertising Bovril and Nestle's Milk along with Michelin Tyres. The adjacent houses have long gone to be replaced by a car sales showroom. The Wheatsheaf public house is visible just behind the two men, (Military gentlemen) on the right of the old photograph.

There is another soldier posing outside the corner shop.

Priory Road

AVONDALE. 1911. HOUSE

CARLTON VILLA 1888

1909

Dyer's Dairies
HIGH CLASS DAIRY PRODUCE
PASTEURISED & TUBERCULIN TESTED MILK
79 PRIORY ROAD
GOSPORT
Telephone 8333

Reflections

PRIORY ROAD IN THE 1940's.

Priory Road in Hardway has featured in several old photographs of Gosport. It is probably due to the previous existence of the Wesleyan Chapel and related Sunday School outings. The Chapel is visible on the right, although today, it has been replaced with newer houses.

As can be seen, Dyers Dairy was located here. Local production of short shelf life products was common in the days prior to refrigerated distribution.

The absence of large numbers of cars is evident. It would be extremely difficult to replicate this today for the photoshoot. The telegraph pole is in its original location, but has been upgraded to newer technology.

House names bearing their date of construction provide a good indicator as to the period when this road in Hardway was developed.

Priory Road
Reflections

PRIORY ROAD, *c.*1908.

In the old, hand coloured photograph, the public house on the left is called the Rose and Crown. This is now the Jolly Roger, which had a brief name change in the 1990's to The Hog's Head and Halibut. As can be seen, the structure has undergone extensive modifications over the past one hundred years, bearing very little resemblence to its former design. Interestingly and probably uniquely in the town, the pub sign is suspended from an overhead line stretching across the road. The flagpole in the centre of the building reflects the nautical location of the pub. The trees on the shoreline were only removed in the 1980's. A lesser number have been replanted in the modern photograph. A horse drawn carriage coming towards the photographer and the posed people, including what appears to be the local postman with his bicycle, outside the public house, all reflect an air of tranquility to the scene. Moby House, the mock Tudor style building, can be seen in the distance in the modern photograph. It was constructed the year after the old photogrpah was taken. It started off life as the White Heather public house. It was used as the control station for the June 1944, D-Day embarkations from the slipway to the right.

Forton Road

Reflections

FORTON ROAD, c.1910.

At the time of the old photograph was taken, the original Spring Gardens were located further along the road behind the fence on the right and on the corner of Parham Road, (shown on the smaller map). The original Spring Gardens were, not surprisingly, previously in Spring Garden Lane, but this area was lost when the Gosport Railway Terminus was built in 1842.

As in most of the old scenes captured of Gosport at the time, the tram features prominently. Here, the number 12, is on its way to the ferry having come from Fareham. It was a bright winter day when the old photograph was taken. The passengers on the exposed upper deck of the tram seem to be enjoying the sunshine. The buildings along the left provide reference points for the picture re-take. Most of the buildings remain today, although the first building from the left has been added in the intervening years. It was used as a furniture warehouse, but was gutted by a fire in 1978.

The Victorian postbox just around the corner is one of the two oldest in the Portsmouth area.

Lee on the Solent

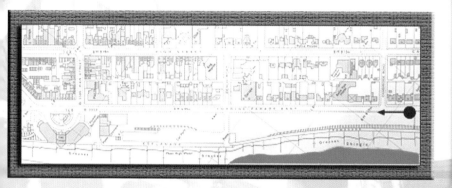

 Reflections

LEE ESPLANADE LOOKING WEST, *c*.1930's.

This old coloured postcard scene looking west along Marine Parade in the 1930's, has not changed greatly over the years at first glance. However, on closer inspection there are some significant changes. Clearly, Lee Tower is no longer there. The road has been widened and the pavement with street lighting laid on the seaward side. One of the buildings on the right in the old view has been converted into the Old Ship public house. Further along, a similar conversion created The Belle View Hotel, which was demolished in 2005.

Lee on the Solent

Reflections

TO LEE TOWER LOOKING WEST, c.1930.

The 43 metre (110 ft) tower built in 1935 in the Art Deco Style, was for many years the key landmark in the area. It was part of a leisure complex which included a cinema, restaurant, bowling alley, dance hall and sun terrace. It could be considered as a forerunner to the Gunwarf Quays development in Portsmouth today. It was demolished in 1971.

The old photograph shows the pier leading out from the tower leisure complex. This was destroyed by fire in 1935. This is shown in the inset view on the old photograph.

The tower was used in World War II as a navigational aid by the German Air Force (Luftwaffe). When this was recognised, the tower was painted in a camouflage design.

In the 1950's during it's peak in popularity Lee Tower, all too often, by some accounts, was the end destination for the bus mystery tours that were popular during that period. The reference point in the faded inserted view, is the roof of the Olympia amusement arcade, which was then the terminus for the railway spur from Gosport. The last train left here in 1935.

It is clear today, how much the promenade has been extended towards the sea.

Reference point

Above, the entrance to the leisure complex in Lee Tower.

ACKNOWLEDGEMENTS

Gosport Library and Museum   The Gosport Society

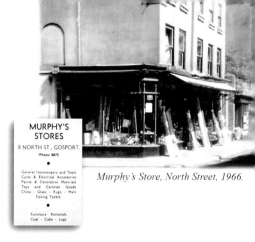

Murphy's Store, North Street, 1966.

PHOTOGRAPH SOURCES

The Gosport Museum   The Stoke Gallery
Mr A C Knight   John Smith
The Gosport Society   Michael White
Ray Stubbington   Craig Moulson
Hampshire Record Office, Hampshire Photographic Project.

ISBN-10: 0-9553876-0-4
ISBN-13: 978-0-9553876-0-9

RESEARCH SOURCES

The Gosport Museum
In Defence of the Realm by John Sadden
Keep the Home Fires Burning by John Sadden
Go Ahead Gosport by Lesley Burton and Beryl Peacy
Gosport- A Century of Change in words and pictures by Lesley Burton and Beryl Peacy
The Book of Gosport by Leslie Burton and Brian Musselwhite

HUHTAMAKI

TAKING PACKAGING FURTHER

My thanks to Huhtamaki for their generous support.

MAPS

Ordnance Survey   © Crown-copyright NC/A7 2006
The Gosport Museum

My gratitude to the photograph sources in permitting the reproduction of their photographs for use in this publication cannot be understated. Also, to those local people who have participated and in some cases, re-enacted the poses from the original photographs I offer my thanks.

A special thanks to my wife Patricia for all her support and encouragement throughout.

Also, many thanks to the following for their contribution.
Alan Brown, Matthew Powell, John Sadden, Norman Edwards, Betty Smith, nee Coyne, Mary Onions, nee Lawrence, Tim Pearce (Southern Gas Neworks), Mulalley Company Limited, Janet Wildman, Karen Flower, Linda Salt, Clare Knowles, Elsie Oakes, nee Williams.